better together*

* This book is best read together, grownup and kid.

 **akidsco.com**

a kids
book
about

a kids book about

POSITIVE MINDSET

by Erin Santamaria

A Kids Co.
Editor Emma Wolf
Designer Jelani Memory
Creative Director Rick DeLucco
Studio Manager Kenya Feldes
Sales Director Melanie Wilkins
Head of Books Jennifer Goldstein
CEO and Founder Jelani Memory

DK
Delhi Technical Team Bimlesh Tiwary Pushpak Tyagi, Rakesh Kumar
Senior Production Editor Jennifer Murray
Senior Production Controller Louise Minihane
Senior Acquisitions Editor Katy Flint
Acquisitions Project Editor Sara Forster
Managing Art Editor Vicky Short
Managing Director, Licensing Mark Searle

First American edition, 2025
Published in the United States by DK Publishing, 1745 Broadway, 20th Floor,
New York, NY 10019

First published in Great Britain in 2025 by
Dorling Kindersley Limited, 20 Vauxhall Bridge Road, London SW1V 2SA
A Penguin Random House Company

The authorised representative in the EEA is
Dorling Kindersley Verlag GmbH. Arnulfstr. 124, 80636 Munich, Germany

A catalog record for this book is available from the Library of Congress.
A CIP catalogue record for this book is available from the British Library.
ISBN: 978-0-2417-4390-4

DK books are available at special discounts when purchased in bulk for sales
promotions, premiums, fund-raising, or education use. For details, contact:
DK Publishing Special Markets, 1745 Broadway, 20th Floor, New York, NY 10019
SpecialSales@dk.com

Printed and bound in China
www.dk.com
akidsco.com

This book was made with Forest
Stewardship Council™ certified
paper – one small step in DK's
commitment to a sustainable future.
**Learn more at www.dk.com/uk/
information/sustainability**

To Jaime and Emma, my little girls.

Remember that even the grayest clouds hold hidden rainbows, and your light and love can brighten the darkest corners of the world.

"You have brains in your head. You have feet in your shoes. You can steer yourself in any direction you choose."—*Oh the Places You'll Go* (Dr.Seuss)

Intro
for grownups

This book is a gentle guide into the colorful world of our minds, illuminating the path to a positive mindset. It's a journey for kids and grownups to explore together, creating an environment where young minds feel safe to share and better understand their thoughts.

Sometimes, our mind can be a playground of joyful ideas. But other times, it may feel more like a maze of confusion or worry. My hope with this book is to turn those mazes into bridges, connecting kids to a mental state where their thoughts can bloom positively.

Parents, guardians, and teachers, this book is your ally. It's a conversation-starter, a tool to empower our kids to recognize and nurture their inner strength. This book is more than just words—it's an invitation to grow a generation of hopeful, confident thinkers.

Do you know how many thoughts go through your mind in 1 single day?

I want you to think of
a number, any number...

SE
THAT WAS

The truth is...

you have

THOUSANDS

of thoughts every day!

CAN YOU BELIEVE IT?!

Thoughts are ideas and opinions which influence how you make decisions based on things you have done before and how you felt doing them.

We can think of thoughts
as a little voice in our heads!

For example, let's say you get invited
to a friend's birthday party.

Do you feel excited? Nervous? Happy?

If you have been to parties before and had the **BEST** time, you'll most likely feel excited about this new invitation.

That little voice might say,

"YAY! THIS WILL BE SO MUCH FUN!"

These kinds of thoughts can make us feel good and push us toward growth and joy.

But, some thoughts make us feel sad, uncertain, and less confident.

DO YOU KNOW WHAT I'M TALKING ABOUT?

The way we think and feel makes up what is called our mindset.

And, I want to teach you how to have a **POSITIVE MINDSET** so that you can be the best version of yourself!

When I was little, I listened to everything that little voice in my head said, because I thought everything it told me was true.

It took me a while, but I finally realized that wasn't always the case!

Have you ever heard the saying, "When life gives you lemons, make lemonade."?

I heard sayings like this all the time, but I didn't really know what they meant!

Now that I'm a grownup, I've learned that a positive mindset is way more than just putting a smile on your face when dealing with a bad situation (aka "making lemonade").

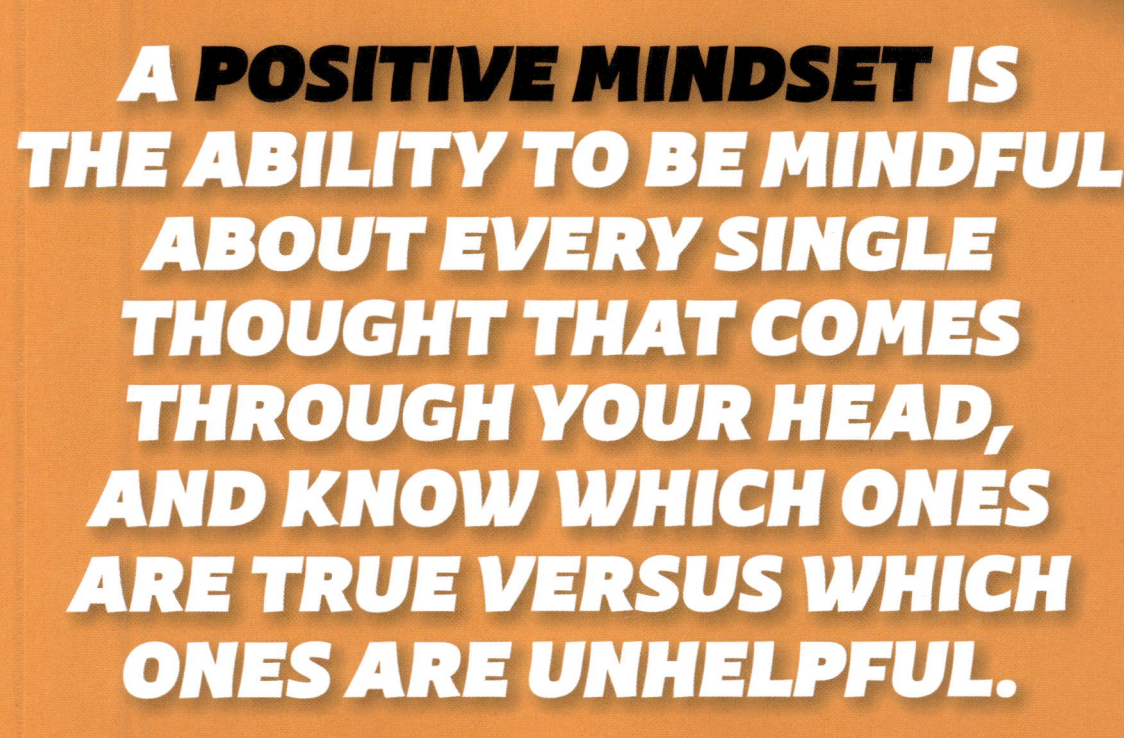

A **POSITIVE MINDSET** IS THE ABILITY TO BE MINDFUL ABOUT EVERY SINGLE THOUGHT THAT COMES THROUGH YOUR HEAD, AND KNOW WHICH ONES ARE TRUE VERSUS WHICH ONES ARE UNHELPFUL.

SO, WHAT DOES THAT MEAN?

Like I said before, we have all kinds of thoughts that run through our heads every day.

Wouldn't it be awesome if we could find a way to make our thoughts generally more positive?

LET'S TRY WITH AN EXAMPLE!

When I was a kid,
I really didn't like math.

So whenever I had a math
test, my negative thoughts
were very strong.

Thoughts like...

 **YOU FAILED THE LAST TEST.**

 **YOU'RE NOT GOOD WITH NUMBERS.**

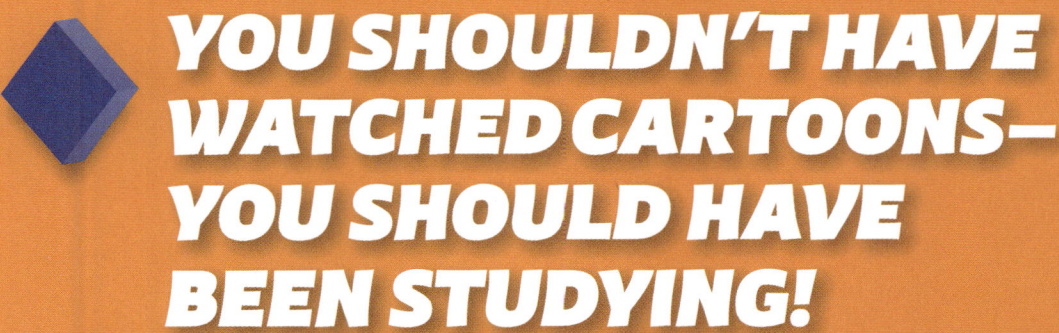 **YOU SHOULDN'T HAVE WATCHED CARTOONS— YOU SHOULD HAVE BEEN STUDYING!**

 **WHY ARE YOU EVEN TRYING?**

Does listening to those thoughts
help someone succeed?

ABSOLUTELY NOT!

Does that mean it's easy to let go of those thoughts?

ABSOLUTELY NOT!

So, what do we do to change from a negative to a positive mindset?

Pretend that your mind is a castle, like one you might read about in a story.

You've worked hard to build this beautiful mind castle, so you hire a guard to protect it and keep you safe from any dragons or monsters (aka negative thoughts).

Now, let's say it's math test day.

You sit down to take the test, and your first thought tries to enter the castle, meeting the guard at the door.

This first thought proclaims,

"YOU WILL FAIL!"

and tries to pass the guard.

But the guard stops the thought and asks whether it's true.

DID YOU STUDY THIS WEEK?

DID YOU ASK FOR HELP WHEN YOU NEEDED IT?

DID YOU WORK THROUGH THE PROBLEMS THAT DIDN'T MAKE SENSE TO YOU?

The more the guard pushes back on the negative thought, the less powerful it becomes.

And once we know that thought isn't true, the guard says,

"THANKS FOR STOPPING BY, BUT YOU'VE GOTTA GO."

Then, another thought approaches the castle.

With a big smile, this one says,
"MAYBE TODAY WILL BE DIFFERENT. YOU'VE WORKED SO HARD ON THIS!"

The guard likes the way this thought feels—warm and supportive—and opens the gate wide so that thought can settle into your mental space.

The more positive thoughts we let in, and the more negative thoughts we keep out...

THE MORE OUR MINDS BECOME A HAPPIER PLACE.

Over time, by better understanding each thought which approaches the castle, that little voice will start to sound more encouraging:

 **YOU ARE WORKING SO HARD.**

 **NOT EVERYTHING WILL BE EASY, BUT STICK WITH IT.**

 **YOU ARE BRAVE FOR DOING THINGS THAT FEEL SCARY.**

 **YOU'VE GOT THIS!**

 **YOU ARE WORTHY NO MATTER WHAT YOUR TEST SCORES ARE.**

And do you wanna
know something cool?

YOU are the ruler of the castle *and*
the guard at the gate—both who
are in charge of your thoughts.

You have control over which thoughts are allowed in and which ones are turned away.

But that doesn't mean it's easy to do every day.

I'm a grownup and still have
to work at this all the time!

Make sure your castle guard is always keeping an eye on any thoughts that come to visit.

IT'S A DAILY PRACTICE!

The castle you've built is beautiful, powerful, and completely you.

It is a fortress against negative thoughts, but allows positive thoughts to enter freely.

AND IT DESERVES YOUR PROTECTION AND CARE.

Outro
for grownups

As this book comes to a close, your positive mindset adventure has just begun. Together, we've learned a real-life technique to help choose our thoughts, just like the wise guard chooses who gets to enter the castle.

Every day offers a new opportunity to use this amazing skill. When a tricky, unwelcome thought knocks at the door of our minds, we can practice allowing only the healthy, helpful ones to take root.

Our minds are incredible fortresses, filled with treasures of thoughts. Keep exploring and guarding them with love. You hold the key to a kingdom of positive thinking.

Thank you for being brave castle guards on this adventure. Ahead lies a bright future filled with joyful thoughts and positivity, all thanks to you!

About The Author

Growing up, Erin (she/her) battled a nagging inner critic, doubting her intelligence and worth. This voice, central to her actions and inactions, seemed unique to her, as conversations with others about negative self-talk were rare.

Through different phases of her life, studying the application of a positive mindset helped grow and shift Erin's perspective dramatically. These breakthroughs revealed that negative self-talk is a common human trait, yet one that can be reshaped with the right tools.

Erin's journey has not been free of obstacles. But, determined to model a positive mindset for her daughters, Erin immersed herself in books about positive thinking, striving to keep the external manifestation of her internal struggles at bay. Her resilience and commitment to positivity are the heart of her message, shared to inspire kids and grownups who need a little nudge in a positive direction.

@rinsreadsforkids

Made to empower.

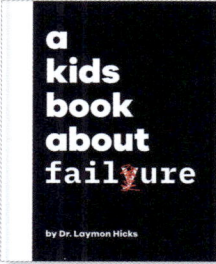

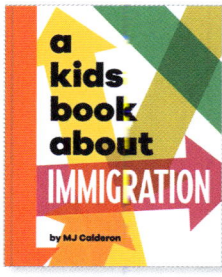

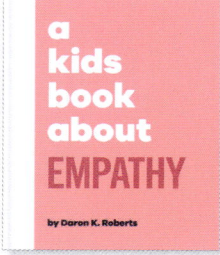

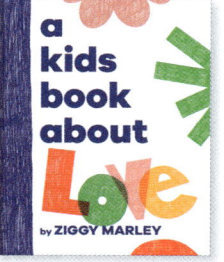
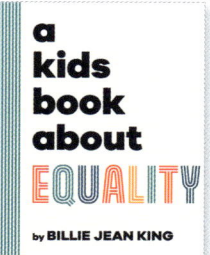

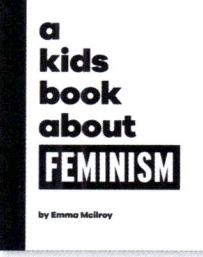
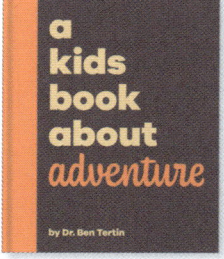

Discover more at akidsco.com